# 50 THINGS YOU SHOULD KNOW ABOUT THE ENVIRONMENT

## by Jen Green

QED

Quarto is the authority on a wide range of topics.
Quarto educates, entertains and enriches the lives of
our readers—enthusiasts and lovers of hands-on living.
www.quartoknows.com

**Design and Editorial:** Tall Tree Ltd
**Consultant:** Professor David M Schultz

Copyright © QED Publishing 2016

First published in the UK in 2016
by QED Publishing
Part of The Quarto Group
The Old Brewery, 6 Blundell Street
London, N7 9BH

A catalogue record for this book is
available from the British Library.

ISBN 978 1 78493 562 7

Printed in China

Words in **bold** are explained
in the glossary on page 78.

# CONTENTS

# INTRODUCTION

The environment is the world around you. It includes all living things as well as non-living features, such as rocks, soil, oceans, rivers and the **atmosphere**. It also includes **climate** and weather. The environment provides everything we need to survive.

## BIOSPHERE

All life on Earth, and the places that support it, are together known as the **biosphere**. Life thrives on Earth in a zone that stretches from the ocean depths up into the lower atmosphere. Living things flourish in the oceans, fresh water and on land, including in caves and in the soil.

## CHANGING CONDITIONS

Planet Earth supports millions of **species**. Conditions in the environment have changed throughout history with Earth experiencing regular periods of warming and cooling. However, conditions are now changing quickly because of the actions of one species – humans.

▼ *More species are found in rainforests than any other land environment, but around the world these forests are disappearing because of human activity.*

▲ Life can thrive in the most surprising places. Tiny organisms called bacteria have even been found living in the super-heated water in this hot spring in Yellowstone National Park, USA.

# EXTREMOPHILES

Most species on Earth are found in lush, fertile places such as rainforests. However, living things called extremophiles can survive in extremely hostile environments, such as hot springs and volcanic vents in the ocean depths.

# SMALL WORLD

Despite the enormous abundance of life on Earth, the biosphere is actually tiny compared to the total size of the planet. The vast majority of Earth – around 99.9 per cent, including the upper atmosphere and fiery interior – is too hot, too cold, or has too little water or oxygen to be able to support life.

▲ Coral reefs are the 'rainforests of the the oceans', supporting thousands of species, and are also under threat.

# Our environment

Planet Earth is one of eight planets circling our local star, the Sun, but it's the only planet that we know for certain supports life. So what exactly is it about Earth's environment that makes it suitable for life to thrive?

Light takes 490 seconds to travel from the Sun to Earth.

## HEAT FROM THE SUN

The Sun provides light and heat energy for life on Earth to flourish. Our planet lies about 150 million kilometres from the Sun – just the right distance to make conditions suitable for life. Any further away and the planet would be frozen; any closer and it would be too hot.

## WATER

Planet Earth is mostly covered by water – a substance essential for life. Life probably began in water 3.8 billion years ago. The oceans, which contain most of the planet's water, also help to control temperatures on Earth.

---

**Atmosphere**
Earth's atmosphere is made up of several gases, forming a protective blanket (see page 8).

**Natural cycles**
Water and carbon cycles help to keep conditions for life stable on Earth (see page 9).

**Land and water**
The rocks of Earth's crust are constantly being recycled. Most of the crust is covered in water (see pages 10–11).

## ATMOSPHERE

Life is also supported by the gases of Earth's atmosphere. Earth is the only planet in the solar system whose atmosphere contains large amounts of oxygen, which many **organisms** need to breathe.

▲ *Earth, with its thick atmosphere and life-filled oceans, as seen from the lifeless surface of the Moon (below).*

## THE MOON

The Moon also helps to keep conditions stable on Earth, allowing life to flourish. Its gravitational pull helps to stabilize the planet's rotation so that it doesn't wobble too much. It also controls the daily rising and falling of Earth's tides.

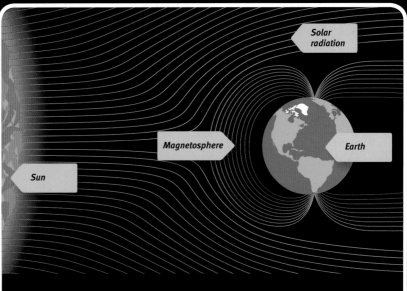

Solar radiation

Magnetosphere

Earth

Sun

## MAGNETIC FIELD

Planet Earth acts like a giant magnet. Molten metal flowing in its core creates a strong magnetic field. This field extends far into space, forming a 'magnetic bubble' called the magnetosphere. This protects the planet from harmful solar and cosmic **radiation**.

**Habitats and biomes**
Earth's surface is divided into a number of environments that support life (see pages 12–13).

**Biodiversity**
There is an enormous variety of life on Earth (see pages 14–15).

**Adaptation and extinction**
Species become suited to their surroundings through adaptations, but can also become extinct (see page 16–17).

# Atmosphere

Earth's atmosphere is a layer of gases about 900 kilometres thick, surrounding the planet like a protective blanket. The gases are densest near the surface and thin out towards space. The atmosphere contains life-giving oxygen. It keeps in warmth and screens the planet from harmful radiation.

## LAYERS

Earth's atmosphere has five main layers. Weather happens in the lowest level, the troposphere. The calm layer above, the stratosphere, contains the ozone layer (see below). Meteors burn up in the mesosphere. Above that is the thermosphere and then the exosphere, which fades off into space.

### EXOSPHERE
Above 640 km

### THERMOSPHERE
85–640 km

### MESOSPHERE
50–85 km

### STRATOSPHERE
18–50 km

### TROPOSPHERE
Up to 18 km

### EARTH

## MAKEUP

Earth's atmosphere is mainly nitrogen (78 per cent) and oxygen (21 per cent). The remaining 1 per cent is mostly argon as well as traces of other gases, including water vapour and methane. Carbon dioxide makes up just 0.03 per cent of the air but is vital for life.

**1%**
Argon, carbon dioxide and trace gases

**78%**
Nitrogen

**21%**
Oxygen

## OZONE AND CO2

Ozone is a form of oxygen. The ozone layer in the atmosphere screens out harmful ultraviolet (UV) radiation from the Sun (see page 45), which otherwise could seriously damage life on Earth.

▶ The ozone layer filters out nearly all the most harmful forms of UV light known as UV-B and UV-C.

UV-A  UV-B  UV-C

*Stratosphere ozone (ozone layer)*

# Natural cycles

Rain falling from clouds is part of the natural cycle that water takes around the planet. As well as water and sunlight, living things need carbon, nitrogen and oxygen. Fortunately, these vital elements are continually being recycled, providing the right conditions for life.

CO2 is released by decomposing matter, animal respiration (breathing) and burning fossil fuels

Plants absorb CO2 and produce oxygen

**Carbon oxygen cycle**

Dead plants decompose, some forming fossil fuels

Animals take in oxygen and breathe out CO2

## CARBON CYCLE

Carbon is vital to life. In the atmosphere it combines with oxygen to form carbon dioxide (CO2). This moves constantly between the air, earth and living things. Plants use CO2 to **photosynthesize** and grow. They release oxygen which animals breathe in. Animals breathe out CO2. When plants die and rot, their carbon forms **fossil fuels**. CO2 is released when these fuels are burned. CO2 is also absorbed and released by the oceans.

## WATER CYCLE

Moisture is always circulating between the air, oceans and land. This cycle is driven by the Sun's energy. Heat from the Sun causes moisture to rise from oceans and lakes in the form of the gas, water vapour. Moist air rises, cools and condenses to form clouds, which later release rain or snow. Some rainwater is absorbed by plants and the soil, the rest drains away into rivers and lakes that empty into the oceans, completing the cycle.

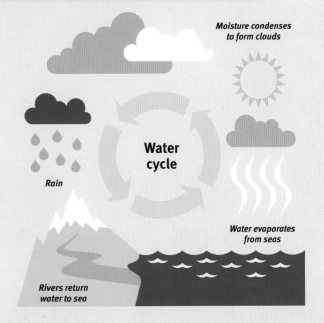

Moisture condenses to form clouds

**Water cycle**

Rain

Water evaporates from seas

Rivers return water to sea

**4**

# Land and water

Seventy-one per cent of Earth is covered by water. Over 97 per cent of this is salty seawater. Less than 3 per cent is fresh water, found underground, in lakes and wetlands, and as solid ice. The oceans are constantly being stirred by waves, tides and currents, while the rocks of the land are continually remade and worn away.

## OCEANS

Earth has five major oceans. Starting with the largest, they are the Pacific, Atlantic, Indian, Southern and Arctic Oceans. There are also many smaller seas. The world's oceans are all interconnected.

▲ A diagram showing Earth's four main layers

Mantle
Outer core
Inner core
Crust

## BELOW THE SURFACE

Beneath both land and seas lies Earth's hard outer crust. Below the crust is a deep layer of hot, molten rock called the mantle, and below that, an outer and inner core of superheated metal. The crust is not one single layer, but is broken into huge chunks called tectonic plates, which ride on the mantle below.

## FROZEN WORLD

Ice covers one-tenth of the land and one-eighth of the oceans. This frozen area is called the cryosphere. It is made up of sea ice, glaciers on mountains and the huge ice caps that cover land in the polar regions.

◄ Ice covers the Arctic Ocean during the winter months.

▲ Water tumbles over the giant Iguazu Falls separating Argentina and Brazil.

## SOIL

Soil is essential for life on land. Soil begins to form when rocks are broken up by **weathering** and **erosion**. Plants take root in the rocky fragments and their rotted remains help to create soil.

## ROCK CYCLE

Rocks may seem fixed, but they are slowly changing all the time. This process is called the rock cycle. Surface rocks are worn away by ice, wind and water to form sediment. This is then compressed on the sea floor to form **sedimentary rock**. At the same time, molten rock erupts through Earth's crust onto the surface, forming **igneous rocks**, while heat and pressure create **metamorphic rocks** underground.

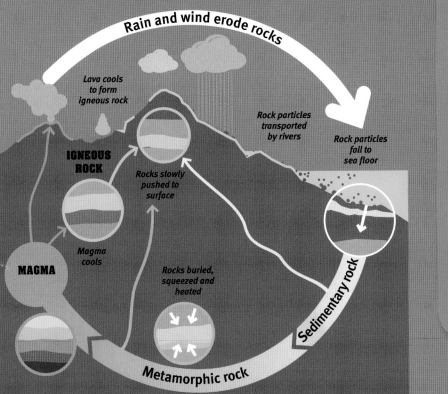

Rain and wind erode rocks

Lava cools to form igneous rock

Rock particles transported by rivers

Rock particles fall to sea floor

IGNEOUS ROCK

Rocks slowly pushed to surface

Magma cools

MAGMA

Rocks buried, squeezed and heated

Sedimentary rock

Metamorphic rock

## CONTINENTS

Twenty-nine per cent of Earth's surface is land, made up of seven large landmasses called continents, and countless smaller islands. The continents aren't fixed in one place, but move very slowly across the globe as the tectonic plates on which they rest are pushed and pulled by currents churning in the mantle.

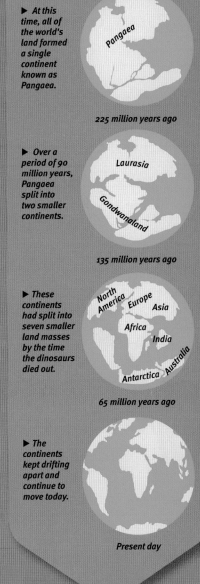

► At this time, all of the world's land formed a single continent known as Pangaea.

Pangaea

225 million years ago

► Over a period of 90 million years, Pangaea split into two smaller continents.

Laurasia

Gondwanaland

135 million years ago

► These continents had split into seven smaller land masses by the time the dinosaurs died out.

North America  Europe  Asia

Africa

India

Antarctica  Australia

65 million years ago

► The continents kept drifting apart and continue to move today.

Present day

# Habitats and biomes

A habitat is a particular place, such as a woodland, that supports living things. Within a woodland are many smaller habitats, such as pools, trees and rotten logs. The largest habitats are called **biomes**. These are huge areas dominated by a certain type of vegetation, such as grass or tropical forest.

▼ 2. The low grasses and shrubs of tundra.

▼ 10. Snow-topped mountains.

## BIOMES

The characteristics of each biome are shaped by a number of factors, including distance from the sea, height of the land and the type of soil. The main one, however, is climate – how hot or cold the area is and how much sunshine and rainfall it receives.

▼ 8. The largest part of the tropical rainforest biome is the Amazon.

## BIOME TYPES

Earth supports 11 main biomes:

1. Polar regions – These are bitterly cold with the land permanently covered by snow.

2. Tundra – The dark, cold winters and brief, cool summers mean that few trees grow. In summer, the ice and snow melt to reveal boggy ground.

3. Boreal forest – Also called the taiga, this is **northern hemisphere** land that stays cold all year round. Most trees are conifers.

4. Temperate woodlands – These have a mild climate with warm summers and cool winters. Most trees are **deciduous**.

5. Chaparral – Enjoying hot, dry summers and mild, wet winters, this region's vegetation is dominated by low-lying shrubs.

6. Temperate grasslands – These have hot summers, cold winters and low rainfall.

7. Tropical grasslands – These are hot and fairly dry with seasonal rains. This type of grassland is also called the savannah.

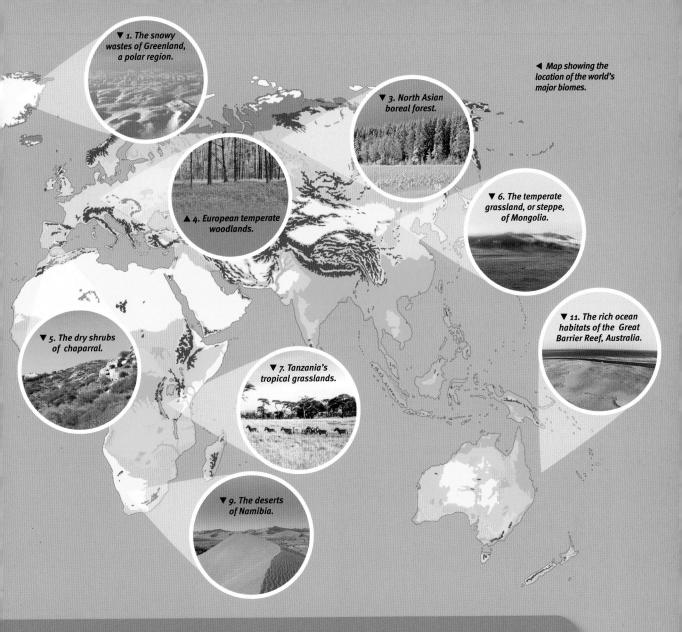

▼ 1. The snowy wastes of Greenland, a polar region.

◄ Map showing the location of the world's major biomes.

▼ 3. North Asian boreal forest.

▼ 6. The temperate grassland, or steppe, of Mongolia.

▲ 4. European temperate woodlands.

▼ 11. The rich ocean habitats of the Great Barrier Reef, Australia.

▼ 5. The dry shrubs of chaparral.

▼ 7. Tanzania's tropical grasslands.

▼ 9. The deserts of Namibia.

8. Tropical rainforests – These grow near the Equator where it is hot and wet all year round. They are very rich in life.

9. Deserts – These dry areas receive less than 25 cm of rain a year and can have extreme temperatures: scorching hot by day but cold at night.

10. Mountains – Conditions in these elevated regions are similar to polar and tundra biomes.

11. Oceans – Oceans contain many different habitats. The main ones are the sunlit upper waters, the mid-waters and the ocean depths. The coral reefs of the tropics contain abundant life.

▲ The ocean's coral reefs support a huge diversity of life.

# Biodiversity

There's a vast number of different species on Earth, ranging from giant blue whales and sequoia trees to microscopic life forms. This huge variety of life is known as **biodiversity**. Nearly two million species have been identified so far, but the actual figure may be over five times larger.

## FIVE KINGDOMS

All the living things on Earth can be divided into five kingdoms: animals, plants, fungi and two types of microscopic life forms – monerans and protists.

## MONERANS

Monerans are tiny, single-celled organisms. They include bacteria, which are abundant, and live in air, water, on land, and inside the bodies of plants and animals.

▶ *Monera bacteria, as seen under a microscope.*

▲ *African elephants are the world's largest species of land animal.*

## PROTISTS

Protists are single-celled life forms, but their cells are more complex than those of monerans. This group includes amoebae and plant-like forms called algae.

Fungi include mushrooms, toadstools and moulds. These many-celled life forms feed by absorbing nutrients from dead plants and animals. They reproduce by releasing spores.

▶ The giant sequoia trees of California, USA, are the world's largest plant species.

▲ Mushrooms can often be found growing in damp, humid habitats.

## PLANTS

Plants include conifers, ferns, mosses and flowering plants. The green parts of plants use energy from sunlight to convert carbon dioxide, water and minerals into food for growth – this process is known as photosynthesis.

## ANIMALS

Animals are complex, multi-celled organisms that eat food for energy and growth. They use their senses to move around and find food. Most reproduce sexually. Around 1.5 million animal species have been identified so far, more than all the other kingdoms put together. Over 95 per cent of animals are invertebrates – animals without a backbone, such as insects, spiders, worms, mollusks and crustaceans. The rest are vertebrates – backboned animals such as mammals, birds, reptiles, amphibians and fish.

# Adaptation

Living things are suited to their environment. This is called **adaptation**. For instance, although jackrabbits and Arctic hares belong to the same group of mammals, they have adapted to live in very different places. Jackrabbits are suited to a hot, dry climate and would not survive in the Arctic. Arctic hares are suited to the frozen tundra and could not survive in a desert.

▼ *Arctic hares have thick fur, which reduces heat loss in a cold climate. Their white colour also provides camouflage, helping the animals to blend in with their environment.*

## HOW SPECIES ADAPT

**Evolution** is the process through which living things adapt to their environment. Within any species, individuals that are well suited to their environment are more likely to survive long enough to breed, and so pass on their characteristics to their offspring. Individuals that are less well suited are more likely to die before breeding. Over time, the whole species evolves to better suit its environment, and new species appear.

▲ *Jackrabbits have fine fur and very long ears which act like radiators, giving off heat. These features help them to keep cool in the desert.*

# Extinction

Just as new species evolve, others die out and become extinct. Since life began on Earth 3.8 billion years ago, as many as 500 million species have evolved. But the vast majority of these have died out. Only a tiny fraction of all the species that have ever existed are alive today. Fossils provide evidence of prehistoric life that is no longer around.

▲ *This is a fossil of an ammonite, a shelled marine creature that became extinct 65 million years ago.*

## WHAT ARE FOSSILS?

Fossils provide a history of life on Earth. These are the remains and impressions of organisms that died thousands (sometimes millions) of years ago. Over a long period, their bones, shells or imprints slowly harden and become preserved in rocks.

## MASS EXTINCTIONS

Most species last only a few million years before dying out. Sometimes, however, a great many species die out at once. This is called a mass extinction. Experts believe this happens when conditions change rapidly – for example when widespread volcanic eruptions result in climate change.

◄ *An artist's impression of the giant asteroid that scientists believe wiped out the dinosaurs.*

## DEATH OF THE DINOSAURS

Fossil evidence suggests there have been at least five major extinctions. Sixty-five million years ago, dinosaurs and many other species died out. Most experts believe a giant rock called an asteroid struck the Earth, causing rapid climate change.

Scientists believe around 97 per cent of all species that have ever existed are now extinct.

# Web of life

An **ecosystem** is a habitat and all the living things that share it. The living things in a particular habitat are known as a community. Plants, animals and other living things interact with their environment, forming a web of life. **Ecologists** study how living things in a community interact with each other and their environment.

## FOOD WEBS

**Herbivores** eat plants and in turn fall prey to predators. Diagrams called food chains show what eats what. Animals eat a varied diet, which makes them part of many food chains. Most environments contain hundreds of food chains, which interlink to form a food web.

▲ A food web shows what eats what in a particular habitat.

## ENERGY PYRAMID

Plants use the Sun's energy to produce food. They are called producers. Plants are eaten by herbivores, which are primary consumers. In turn, these may be eaten by predators, which are secondary consumers – and so on up the food chain to top predators. At every stage in the chain some energy is lost, which produces a pyramid shape.

◄ An energy pyramid showing the flow of energy from one feeding level to the next.

Tertiary consumers (top predators)

Secondary consumers (predators)

Primary consumers (herbivores)

Primary producers (such as plants and algae)

All living things play a particular role in their environment. This is called a niche. However, only one species can fill a niche in any habitat – if there were two, they would compete for the same food. For instance, anteaters occupy a certain niche in South America – they eat ants and termites. In places where there are no anteaters, other animals fill this niche.

▲ A pack of wolves chases a bull elk in Yellowstone National Park.

# KEYSTONE SPECIES

Animals called keystone species play a vital role in their environment. One example is the wolf – a top predator. Wolves affect many links in food chains below them. They keep down numbers of plant-eaters that might otherwise graze habitats bare. In this way they help nature to stay in balance. They also prey on weak and sickly individuals, which helps to keep prey populations at numbers the habitat can support.

# Human impact

Environments on Earth are always changing. Species that cannot adapt to the changes die out. But in the last few centuries, environments have been dramatically transformed by humans. As human numbers rise, so our use of Earth's resources increases. This is putting pressure on habitats and wildlife, threatening the existence of many living things.

## WATER SHORTAGES

The pressures put on resources by people are shown by the global use of water. Of the 3 per cent of the total amount of water that is fresh, just 1 per cent is available to us. And 0.7 per cent of that is used for watering crops.

## POPULATION GROWTH

In 1830, there were around one billion people on Earth. Just 100 years later, the figure had doubled, and by 2012 the population was seven billion. Experts predict that by 2050 the planet may be home to as many as nine billion people. As the human population grows, we need ever-increasing amounts of resources, such as food, water, land and fuel.

**Habitat loss**
Human activity has resulted in the loss of many natural habitats (see pages 22–23).

**Deforestation**
Rainforests are being destroyed at an alarming rate (see pages 24–25).

**Impact of farming**
Across the world, farming seriously affects habitats (see page 26).

**Introductions**
Species introduced to habitats have an impact on native wildlife (see page 27).

# SPREAD OF HUMANS

The human species, *Homo sapiens*, emerged in Africa about 200,000 years ago. Gradually people spread to other regions. About 150,000 years ago, humans moved out of Africa to settle in Asia and Europe. Later people reached Australia and then the Americas. The last continent to be discovered was Antarctica, where the first settlements date from the 1960s.

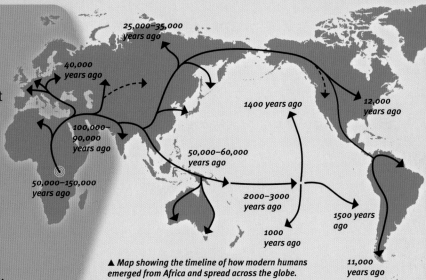

25,000–35,000 years ago

40,000 years ago

100,000–90,000 years ago

50,000–150,000 years ago

50,000–60,000 years ago

1400 years ago

12,000 years ago

2000–3000 years ago

1000 years ago

1500 years ago

11,000 years ago

▲ Map showing the timeline of how modern humans emerged from Africa and spread across the globe.

# INDUSTRIAL REVOLUTION

Human impact on the planet has grown considerably since the **Industrial Revolution**, which began in the late 1700s. Mass production began in factories, which were soon built in many parts of the world. Industrialization continues today, increasing demands on fuel and natural resources.

▼ German workers in one of the thousands of new factories built during the Industrial Revolution.

**Hunting and collecting**

In many places, wildlife is threatened by hunting and overcollecting (see pages 28–29).

**Harvesting the oceans**

Overfishing threatens wildlife in the oceans (see page 30).

**Going, going, gone**

Many species are at risk of dying out (see page 31).

# Habitat loss

All living things need a clean, healthy environment. However, all over the world, wild habitats are being altered or destroyed to make way for cities, farms, roads, mines and other developments. This is called habitat loss, and it's the single biggest threat to biodiversity worldwide.

## GROWING CITIES

Across the world, the only habitats that are expanding are urban landscapes. Large cities cover hundreds of square kilometres, while roads, railways, car parks and airports take up yet more land. Urban areas now cover three per cent of Earth's land – that may not sound a lot, but cities draw natural resources from a huge area, and so have a huge impact. Species such as foxes, pigeons and some wild plants thrive in these concrete jungles, but cities cannot support the biodiversity of wild habitats.

## EXPANDING FARMLANDS

As the human population increases, so more and more land is needed to grow food. This means that farmland expands at the expense of forests and grasslands. In the 1800s, huge swathes of the American prairies and Asian grasslands were ploughed up to grow crops. Farmlands now cover over 40 per cent of Earth's land – a vast area that once supported a wealth of life.

# MINING

Quarrying and mining provide rocks and minerals, which are used to make a huge range of goods, from cars to computers. Coal and oil are mined to provide energy. Metals and gemstones, such as gold, silver and diamonds, are used in industry and to make jewellery. However mining, quarrying and drilling for oil destroy ecosystems and also create pollution (see page 48).

▶ Large open-cast mines inflict great damage to the environment, stripping areas of vegetation.

## IMPACT ON NATURE

When wetlands are drained to create new land for farms and cities, aquatic plants and animals, such as fish, frogs and beavers, lose their habitats. These species are adapted to their environment, so they cannot just move elsewhere. Likewise, coastal plants and animals lose their habitat when new resorts, towns and marinas are built along the shore.

◀ Combine harvesters clear a field of wheat in one of the vast farms covering much of the USA.

▶ Amphibians, such as this green tree frog, are particularly vulnerable to habitat loss.

## 12 Deforestation

Lush tropical rainforests are incredibly rich in life, supporting thousands of species. Yet over half of these amazing forests have been felled in the past 150 years. This destruction is called deforestation, and if it continues, only pockets of forest could be left by 2100.

### BIODIVERSITY

Tropical forests cover just a fraction of Earth's surface but may be home to half of all land species. Over 400 different trees can exist in 1 hectare of tropical forest – that compares to around 12 species in temperate forests. Rainforests support thousands of invertebrates, mammals, amphibians and birds.

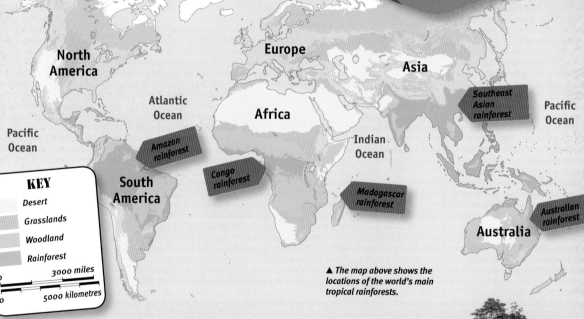

**North America**

**Europe**

**Asia**

Atlantic Ocean

**Africa**

Southeast Asian rainforest

Pacific Ocean

Pacific Ocean

Amazon rainforest

Indian Ocean

**KEY**

Desert
Grasslands
Woodland
Rainforest

0    3000 miles
0    5000 kilometres

**South America**

Congo rainforest

Madagascar rainforest

Australian rainforest

**Australia**

▲ The map above shows the locations of the world's main tropical rainforests.

### WHERE DO RAINFORESTS GROW?

Rainforests grow in a belt on either side of the Equator, where the climate is warm and wet. The largest is the Amazon rainforest in South America. In 1970, the Brazilian Amazon rainforest covered 4 million square kilometres, but huge areas have been felled in the last 40 years, and only 3.3 million square kilometres were left by 2014.

▲ Rainforest being felled in Borneo.

## WHY ARE RAINFORESTS IMPORTANT?

Rainforests have been called Earth's 'green lungs' because they top up oxygen in the atmosphere. They also absorb huge amounts of carbon dioxide. In addition, by soaking up rainwater and releasing it slowly, they recycle moisture, bringing rain to nearby lands.

▶ A blue-and-yellow macaw flies over an area of cleared forest.

## DWINDLING FORESTS

Tropical rainforests are disappearing for many reasons. They are logged for their valuable timber and for fuel. They are cleared to make way for new mines and towns, and particularly for farms, plantations and cattle ranches. However, forest soil is poor and unsuitable for farming. After a few years the land becomes infertile, and farmers move on to clear a new patch of forest.

▶ Cattle graze on deforested land in Pantanal, Brazil.

## FRAGMENTATION

Some areas of forest have been cleared completely. Elsewhere, small pockets of forest remain, but the wildlife is isolated. Animals cannot move freely through the forest to find food and to mate. This problem is called fragmentation.

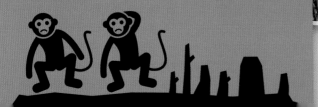

# Impact of farming

In prehistoric times people lived by hunting and gathering wild foods. Now almost all the food we eat comes from crops and domestic livestock. Farming is the world's biggest industry but it has a huge impact on the natural world.

▶ The use of large fields in modern farming means there are fewer hedges to protect wildlife.

## LOSS OF HEDGES

A century ago, the British countryside was a patchwork of small fields divided by hedges, which sheltered wildlife. But in the 1960s and 1970s many hedges were torn up to make larger fields. The biodiversity of the countryside was sacrificed to cultivate crops.

▼ Some hedges do survive in parts of the UK even though they are in decline.

## HOW FARMING BEGAN

Farming began around 11,000 years ago as people began to grow crops and breed livestock. The birth of farming allowed people to settle in one place rather than move around in search of food. This allowed the first towns to develop, followed by the first cities.

▶ The sickle, a short-handled agricultural tool, has been used by farmers for thousands of years to cut down crops.

▲ British wildlife that depends on hedges, such as hedgehogs, has found it harder to thrive.

## EROSION

When wild habitats are converted to farmland, the natural vegetation is removed. Without trees and plants to keep the soil in place, the land is at risk of erosion. In the 1800s, the American prairies were ploughed up to grow wheat. But in the 1930s, years of drought turned the soil to dust, which blew away on the wind. Land that was once rich in life became a barren desert. It took years for the region to recover.

▼ A dust storm engulfs a Texan town in 1936.

# Introductions

Introduced species are living things that do not belong in an environment. They are there because people have introduced them, either on purpose or by accident. Introduced species such as crops are very useful, but other newcomers become invasive – they harm ecosystems or native species.

▶ *Invasive species, such as rabbits in Australia (top), water hyacinths in Africa (right), tiger mussels in the USA (lower right) and grey squirrels in the UK (below), have driven out local species.*

## WHY ARE SPECIES INTRODUCED?

New species are brought in for a number of reasons:

- 🌐 Crops have been introduced all over the world to provide food.

- 🌐 Animals such as cows, sheep, domestic fowl and rabbits have been introduced for food.

- 🌐 Attractive plants, trees and animals such as songbirds are added to 'improve' the scenery.

- 🌐 Dogs and cats arrive as pets.

- 🌐 Species such as rats and snakes arrive accidentally, as 'stowaways' on ships, trucks and planes.

## IMPACT

Both deliberate and accidental introductions can disturb the balance of nature in their new habitat. Non-native predators such as cats and rats prey on native birds. Introduced plant-eaters outcompete native herbivores. Rabbits introduced to Australia for meat have nibbled grasslands bare. Amazon water hyacinths introduced to decorate North American lakes now smother waterways.

Introduced to the USA from Asia in the 1930s, the kudzu vine can grow over 30 cm a day.

Sharks kill 10 to 20 people each year, but people kill thousands of sharks every day.

28

# Hunting and collecting

People have hunted animals since prehistoric times. But when there were just a few people armed with spears and bows, hunting had little effect on prey numbers. The invention of the rifle stacked the odds against the hunted. Illegal hunting now threatens the survival of many animals, including tigers, elephants and rhinos. Other species are rare because they are captured and sold alive. This practice threatens plants, such as orchids, and some reptiles.

## BUSHMEAT

Almost all our meat in developed countries comes from farmed livestock. But in regions such as Africa, wild animals are still hunted for food – this is known as bushmeat. Hunting for bushmeat threatens the survival of some antelopes, and even chimps and gorillas.

▶ *Common to much of Africa, the roan antelope is hunted both for bushmeat and sport.*

## FUR, IVORY AND SHELLS

Animals are also killed for their body parts, such as skin, shells and feathers. Leopards are killed for their spotted fur coats. Crocodile skins are made into belts and bags. Turtle shells are used as ornaments. Elephants and rhinos are butchered for their tusks and horns. Body parts of tigers, rhinos and seahorses are used in traditional Chinese medicine. Many of these practices are now illegal, but they still go on.

▼ Humans kill more than 100 million sharks every year.

# DANGEROUS ANIMALS

Powerful or deadly animals, including tigers, bears, sharks and poisonous snakes, are often killed out of fear. In reality, tigers and bears pose little threat to humans, but they do need a large space to hunt in. As farms and urban areas expand, there is less and less wild land where animals can roam freely.

## SPORT HUNTING

Hunting for pleasure, known as 'sport hunting', has gone on since ancient times. In the 1800s, wealthy Europeans travelled to Africa and India to shoot lions and tigers, hugely reducing their populations. Sport hunting is still widely practised, but nowadays, when carefully regulated, it can help to fund conservation and reserves (see page 35).

▶ A combination of habitat loss and hunting means there are now fewer than 4000 tigers left in the wild.

▼ Many types of turtle, including this river terrapin, are killed for their shells.

## OVERCOLLECTING

Many plants and animals are worth more alive than dead. They are captured from the wild and sold as pets or specimens. Overcollecting threatens some songbirds, monkeys, snakes, spiders and plants such as orchids. Live species can be delicate and often do not survive the journey.

▶ Overcollection has made this US orchid, the Californian lady's slipper, extremely rare.

# Harvesting the oceans

▲ *Seabirds follow the long nets of a shrimp trawler in the Netherlands, hoping to steal some of the catch.*

Fish and shellfish are a major source of food worldwide. Small-scale fishing does little harm to fish stocks, but commercial fishing fleets gather such large hauls that some seas have very few fish left.

## COD COLLAPSE

The Grand Banks off Newfoundland, Canada, were once a rich fishing ground for cod. Fishing fleets came from far and wide to collect the fish, and cod stocks plummeted. In 1992, the cod **fishery** collapsed, affecting marine food chains and putting many local fishermen out of work.

▼ *Cod being unloaded in Iceland, which, like many other countries, has introduced strict fishing limits in recent years to preserve its stocks.*

## MODERN FISHING

• • • • • • • • • • • • • •

Commercial fishing fleets use sonar (sound waves) to pinpoint shoals of fish. Deep-sea trawlers use huge nets that can catch 100 tonnes of fish at once. Fish stocks plummet when not enough fish are left to breed – this is called overfishing. Many countries now limit the numbers of fish that can be caught by fishermen to allow fish stocks to recover.

## BYCATCH

Animals such as dolphins and turtles can get trapped in fishing nets and drown. Their bodies are just dumped in the oceans – this waste is known as bycatch. Some fishing boats use special nets that allow dolphins, turtles and young fish to escape.

◄ *A shark has been accidentally caught as bycatch in a haul of shellfish and lobster.*

Around 150 million tonnes of fish are netted annually from the world's oceans.

# Going, going, gone

**Across the world, many plants and animals are now very rare because of the activities of people. Habitat loss, hunting, introductions and climate change (see pages 58–67) are the main threats that are putting many species at risk.**

(see pages 58–67)

▲ *The golden toad was once common to a small area of Costa Rica, but became extinct in the 1990s, probably because of climate change.*

## SIXTH EXTINCTION?

Fossil evidence shows there have been at least five natural mass extinctions in the past. Now scientists fear a sixth extinction is underway – this time caused by humans. Experts say dozens of species are now dying out each day.

## GONE FOREVER

When you hear the word 'extinction', you may think of the dodo. This flightless bird from the island of Mauritius was wiped out by hungry sailors in the 1600s. Other extinctions include that of a large marine mammal called Steller's sea cow in the 1700s and the American passenger pigeon in the 1900s. Both were wiped out by hunters.

▲ *A model of the now extinct dodo, a flightless member of the pigeon family.*

## IN DANGER

Black rhinos, Ethiopian wolves and the world's largest flower, rafflesia, are among Earth's most endangered plants and animals. Giant pandas and mountain gorillas are also on the danger list. If we don't take care of these, and many other species, they could become extinct like the dodo.

◄ *There are just 4000 black rhinos left living in the wild in Africa.*

**Scientists believe at least 2000 species become extinct every year.**

# 18 Conservation

People now live all over the planet, where the building of cities, transport systems and the like has drastically changed the natural environment. But many people think we also have a responsibility to look after nature. Conservation is the movement to protect the natural world. Conservationists raise awareness of environmental issues and work to set up wildlife sanctuaries and save rare species.

## ENVIRONMENTALISM

The conservation movement is also called environmentalism. The 1970s and 1980s saw the rise of 'green' political parties in countries such as Germany and New Zealand, which campaigned on environmental issues.

## SAVE OUR SKINS

Conservationists work to change how people think about environmental matters. In the mid-1900s, fur coats made from seal and mink were popular. In the 1970s, conservation groups filmed fur hunters killing seals. The films convinced many people that it was wrong to kill animals for fur.

◀ *Most of the harp seals killed for their fur are three weeks to three months old.*

---

**Saving habitats**
National parks have been set up across the world to protect natural environments (see pages 34–35).

**Protecting coasts and wetlands**
National laws and international agreements help to protect wildlife (see page 36).

**Managing parks and reserves**
Parks need careful management and regulation to maintain their environments (see page 37).

The Scottish-American naturalist John Muir (1838–1914) was a pioneer of conservation. Muir believed that nature was not just something to be tamed, but needed protection. He was concerned that species such as the American bison, which had once been abundant, could be hunted to extinction. Muir helped found the Sierra Club, which campaigned to create national parks across the USA.

◀ *The efforts of the naturalist John Muir eventually led to the creation of Sequoia and Yosemite National Parks in 1890.*

# CONSERVATION GOALS

The main aim of conservation is the careful management of the Earth's natural resources.

## WILDLIFE

Wildlife, particularly rare species, needs to be protected from hunting and poaching.

▲ *Elephants, which are often hunted for their ivory, in the protected Tarangire National Park, Tanzania.*

## HABITATS

Conservationists campaign for laws to both protect and restore habitats where species can live and thrive without interference from humans.

▲ *A member of the Clean & Green environmental group plants a tree in Los Angeles as part of a habitat regeneration programme.*

**Conserving wildlife**
Conservationists employ numerous strategies to protect species (see pages 38–39).

**Assessing risk**
The IUCN publishes a list of endangered animals every five years (see page 40).

**Back from the brink**
Drastic steps are sometimes needed to save critically endangered animals (see page 41).

# Saving habitats

The best way to preserve wildlife is to protect the environment. Reserves and national parks offer this protection. National parks are usually large, scenic areas where building and development are banned. Reserves are often smaller areas created to protect a certain rare animal or plant.

## FIRST NATIONAL PARK

In the late 1800s, US conservationists realized that wild environments needed protection. In 1872, the world's first national park, Yellowstone, was established in the Rocky Mountains. Many countries followed this example. The first national parks in the UK opened in the 1950s. Today, about 12 per cent of Earth's surface is protected by national parks.

## HOW MUCH LAND?

A leading conservation organization suggests that at least 10 per cent of every country should be protected. Germany, China and New Zealand, for example, exceed this target, while other countries fall short.

## WORLD'S LARGEST PARKS

Northeast Greenland National Park is the world's largest. Established in 1974, it covers 927,000 square kilometres. The Wrangell–St. Elias in Alaska is the largest park in the USA, while the Kavango–Zambezi Conservation Area is a vast reserve in Africa.

Wood Buffalo National Park in Canada covers an area larger than Switzerland.

# GAME RESERVES

Hunting has wiped out many species, but it can also play a role in conservation. In South Africa, for example, hunters visit game reserves to bag trophies. The fees they pay are used to run the reserves and protect the environment. Game reserves cover more land than national parks in South Africa. In North America, duck hunters help to preserve wetlands.

▲ Paulet Island in Antarctica supports a very large breeding colony of 100,000 pairs of Adélie penguins.

◄ A curious elephant approaches a jeep on a game reserve in Botswana, Africa.

## ANTARCTICA

Antarctica, the world's fourth-largest continent, is a wildlife sanctuary. It is not a national park because no country owns it. By the mid-1900s many countries had claimed land in Antarctica, but in 1959 they agreed to set their claims aside, and the whole continent was protected. No development is allowed and the surrounding seas are a sanctuary for whales and other wildlife.

## BIODIVERSITY HOTSPOTS

Some parts of the world contain far more biodiversity than others. In 1988, ecologists drew up a map of 35 'biodiversity hotspots', rich in unique wildlife. These hotspots, which include the Caribbean and New Zealand, cover just 3 per cent of Earth's land, but are home to over 40 per cent of animal species.

▲ The Grand Prismatic Spring is one of the highlights of Yellowstone National Park, USA. Its amazing colours are caused by coloured microbes living in the hot spring water.

▶ Map showing biodiversity hotspots across the globe, most of which are in the ocean.

# Protecting coasts and wetlands

Not all parks and reserves are on dry land. Wetlands, such as lakes and swamps, are also protected. Marine reserves protect coastal habitats, islands and coral reefs.

▼ *The Great Barrier Reef off northeastern Australia stretches for 2600 kilometres. It is home to 350 species of coral, 4000 different molluscs and 1500 types of fish.*

## CORAL REEFS

Coral reefs are habitats rich in wildlife. They cover only a fraction of the oceans, but are home to one-third of all marine species. These reefs resemble rock, but are actually made of the chalky skeletons of anemone-like creatures called coral polyps. When these animals die, their skeletons build up to form the reef.

## ISLAND DRAGON

Remote islands are often home to species that are found nowhere else. Such species are called endemics. The island of Komodo in Indonesia is home to the Komodo dragon. Komodo and the surrounding seas are a national park.

▲ *The Komodo dragon is the largest species of lizard on Earth.*

## EVERGLADES

The Florida Everglades is a wetland in the southeastern USA. Covering more than 2000 square kilometres, this national park protects alligators and many water birds.

◀ *An alligator at the Darling National Wildlife Refuge in the Florida Everglades, USA.*

# Managing parks and reserves

National parks and reserves have two main aims: to protect nature and allow people to enjoy it. Sometimes these two aims conflict – for example, when large numbers of visitors threaten to spoil the wild, scenic beauty of a park.

▲ Parks and reserves aim to attract visitors so that people can explore nature. However, too many visitors can cause problems, such as paths being worn away.

## PARKS AND PEOPLE

In the USA, very few people live in parks. They have been set up as 'wilderness areas'. However, British parks have towns, villages and even power plants. The park authorities must manage visitors and natural resources, and also help provide jobs and housing for the people that live there.

## PARK RULES

Parks and reserves have rules to protect nature. Development is carefully controlled. People are encouraged to leave their cars to reduce pollution, and explore by bus, by bike, on foot or on horseback. No one is allowed to drop litter, pick plants or disturb animals. 'Take nothing but photos. Leave nothing but footprints' is one of the mottos of the conservation movement.

DO NOT FEED THE WILD WATERFOWL

Porfavor não deêm de comer aos patos

# Conserving wildlife

Imagine a world without tigers, rhinos and pandas. It could soon become a reality if we don't act to save these creatures. Luckily conservationists have persuaded many countries to pass laws to protect wildlife.

## BIODIVERSITY CONVENTION

The International Union for Conservation of Nature (IUCN) is a leading conservation organization. It has experts from 1000 environmental groups. In 1992, the IUCN drew up a major treaty called the Convention on Biological Diversity. Today, 150 nations have signed this pledge to protect wildlife.

## CITES AGREEMENT

In 1975, the IUCN drafted a landmark treaty banning trade in rare species – the Convention on International Trade in Endangered Species, commonly known as CITES. As well as live plants and animals, the treaty also bans trade in furs, ivory and turtle shells.

▼ This illegal stock of ivory was taken from African elephants by poachers.

## POACHING

Unfortunately, illegal poaching continues despite CITES. The rarer the plant or animal, the higher the price it fetches on the illegal market. For example, one rhino horn is worth more than a year's wages in Africa. Rhinos and other animals at risk from poaching are kept in fenced reserves patrolled by guards.

◄ This rhino's horns have been sawn off by conservationists to protect it from poachers.

Conservationists draw up plans to protect rare species. The first step is to find out about the species' needs in terms of habitat. Radio collars or tracking devices are fitted to animals such as big cats, birds and whales to find out their range – the area in which they roam.

▲ This rhino is having a transmitter chip inserted into its horn to track it and help protect it against poachers.

▶ The Arabian oryx is native to the steppes of the Arabian peninsula where it was almost hunted to extinction.

## SAVE THE PANDA

The giant panda is an international symbol of conservation. Hunting and habitat loss brought this Chinese forest bear close to extinction. A captive breeding programme has since helped boost its numbers, but has been very expensive. There is little safe habitat left in which to release these animals, and many people think that money spent on captive breeding would have been better spent saving the bears' habitat.

## CAPTIVE BREEDING

Rare animals are sometimes bred in captivity to increase their numbers. Captive breeding saved an antelope called the Arabian oryx, which was almost extinct by 1970. The few that remained were captured and bred in zoos, and later some were released into the wild. There are now about 7000 oryx, including 1000 in the wild.

(23) ▶

# Assessing risk

**Around the world, many living things are now at risk of extinction. But exactly how rare are they? Experts must assess how many are left, and the threats they face, so the right steps can be taken to ensure their survival.**

## THE RED LIST

The IUCN's Red List details the conservation status of all animals and plants. Experts place each species in one of seven categories, from 'least concern' to 'extinct'. IUCN scientists have now assessed 59,000 species. They believe that 19,000 species are at risk of dying out before 2100 unless action is taken.

**EX** **EW** **CR** **EN** **VU** **NT** **LC**

Extinct | Extinct in the wild | Critically endangered | Endangered | Vulnerable | Near threatened | Least concern

▲ All living species are placed in one of seven categories by the Red List.

▶ The percentage of species in each group that are categorized as critically endangered (red), endangered (orange), or vulnerable (yellow).

30%
25%
20%
15%
10%
5%
0%

Mammals Birds Reptiles Amphibians Fishes Insects Molluscs Plants

## GORILLAS IN DANGER

Very rare species are classed as critically endangered. An example is the mountain gorilla of central Africa, which is threatened by deforestation, war, disease and hunting. Experts believe fewer than 800 are left in the wild.

◀ An adult female mountain gorilla and infant in Rwanda, Africa.

# Back from the brink

A species is critically endangered when only a few hundred are left. The race is then on to protect its habitat and ban hunting or collecting. Sometimes drastic action has to be taken.

▲ 'Lonesome George' was the last member of his subspecies of tortoise – he died in 2012.

## SAVING WHALES

Whaling (hunting whales for their oil, meat or bones) was a major industry from the 1700s to mid-1900s. By 1960, species such as blue and grey whales faced extinction. In the 1970s the conservation group Greenpeace launched a campaign to save whales. It confronted the whaling ships to highlight what was happening. As a result many people persuaded their governments that whaling should stop.

## REMOVING SPECIES

The Galápagos Islands off Ecuador are home to rare and unique giant tortoises and sea-going lizards. To ensure their survival, introduced goats have been removed to leave grazing areas for the tortoises. Introduced rats and cats have also been removed – they were preying on the reptiles' eggs and young.

▼ The tuatara is such an ancient species it is known as a living fossil.

▲ Humpback whales were almost driven to extinction before hunting stopped in 1966. Today they number about 80,000.

### RELOCATION

In New Zealand, the tuatara is the only surviving species of a type of reptile that flourished around 200 million years ago. These reptiles have been moved from the mainland to a few small offshore islands to protect them from non-native predators such as rats.

The blue whale, the largest species that has ever lived, is classed as endangered.

# Waste and pollution

All living things need a clean environment to flourish. Yet habitats throughout the world are exposed to pollution that harms plants, animals and people. Any waste that ends up in the environment can be called pollution. Cities, farms, factories, cars and power plants all produce harmful pollution. Sadly, traces of pollution have even reached remote places, such as Antarctica and the bottom of the oceans.

## TYPES OF POLLUTION

Pollution can be a gas, a liquid or a solid. Smog, bad smells, sewage and litter are all types of pollution. Pollution can spread through the air, water or soil. Substances that cause pollution are called pollutants. Pollution is caused by waste that is dumped deliberately, and also by accidents such as oil spills.

▶ A coal-fired power plant belches smoke containing the gas carbon dioxide. This traps heat in the atmosphere, warming up the planet.

**Air pollution**
Pollutants in the air harm the atmosphere (see page 44).

**Ozone loss**
The ozone layer protects us from harmful radiation (see page 45).

**Acid rain**
Pollution from vehicles and industry makes rain acidic (see page 46).

**Farm chemicals**
Fertilizers and pesticides pollute water and soil (see page 47).

▼ A large passenger plane roars in to land just above a street in London, UK.

## LIGHT POLLUTION

Artificial light is a growing form of pollution all over the world. The bright lights of cities can disturb animals that are active at night, such as bats. When baby turtles hatch out at night on beaches, they head for the glimmering water. The lights of hotels can make them lose their way.

## NOISE POLLUTION

Noise can be a form of pollution. People living near airports may be disturbed by the sound of planes taking off and landing. In the oceans, whales and dolphins use sound to communicate, find food and navigate. The noise of ships' engines can disrupt their communication and send them off course.

▲ A satellite view of North and South America shows the continents' cities brightly lit at night.

🌎 **Water pollution**
Pollutants cause problems in lakes, rivers and oceans (see pages 48–49).

🌎 **Tackling pollution**
There are many different ways of clearing up pollution (see pages 50–51).

🌎 **What a waste!**
Rubbish can cause pollution if not properly disposed of (see pages 52–53).

🌎 **Does it rot?**
Some materials rot quickly, while others decay very slowly (see page 54).

# Air pollution

## SMOG

Smog is a dirty brown haze that pollutes the air in cities. It forms when waste gases from cars and industry react with sunlight. Smog is worst in calm, sunny weather when there is no wind to disperse it. It can cause coughs, asthma and lung infections. Some people in cities wear masks to filter the air they breathe.

The balance of gases in Earth's atmosphere has stayed the same for many thousands of years. But now human activity is disturbing this balance by adding pollutants. Air pollution is spread by the wind – which can also help to disperse it. Air pollution harms living things, including people.

◀ *A volcano in Japan sends a great plume of polluting smoke up into the sky following an eruption in 2009.*

## NATURAL POLLUTION

Not all pollution is man-made. Volcanic eruptions shoot clouds of ash and gas high into the air. This pollution can block out sunlight and cause cooler temperatures, but the effects don't usually last long.

## CAUSES

Homes, offices, factories, cars, planes and power plants all produce waste gases as they burn fuels such as oil and coal. Since the Industrial Revolution, Western nations have produced huge amounts of pollution. As more countries industrialize, more pollution is pumped into the atmosphere.

*The three smoggiest cities in the world are all located in India.*

▶ *Car exhaust fumes are a major source of air pollution.*

# Ozone loss

Ozone gas exists in several levels of the atmosphere. Low-level ozone can be harmful, but a layer of ozone high in the stratosphere shields us from harmful ultraviolet (UV) rays in sunlight. However, this vital barrier can be damaged by air pollution.

## UV DANGER

Ultraviolet radiation is harmful to plants, animals and people. It can cause skin cancer, eye cataracts and other health problems. Because of ozone loss, it's vital to apply suntan lotion whenever you're in the sun, and wear sunglasses to protect your eyes.

In 2015, the ozone hole was roughly the size of North America.

## THINNING OZONE

In the 1980s, scientists discovered that the ozone layer had become thinner. The loss was greatest over the polar regions, where ozone 'holes' were appearing each summer. But what was causing the problem?

▶ A false-colour image of the hole (the blue area) in the ozone layer that appeared over Antarctica in 2015. The hole is slowly getting smaller.

## FIXING A HOLE

Scientists soon realized that the ozone layer was being damaged by chemicals called chlorofluorocarbons – CFCs for short. These were used in fridges, aerosol cans and plastics. In 1987 at an international conference in Montreal, Canada, governments agreed to phase out the use of CFCs to allow the ozone layer to recover.

◀ Modern aerosol cans no longer use CFCs.

# Acid rain

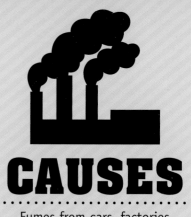

Some forms of air pollution affect the whole environment, passing from the air to water and soil, and affecting plants, animals and people. Acid rain is an example.

## CAUSES

Fumes from cars, factories and power stations contain pollutants. These drift in the air and are absorbed by the tiny water drops that gather to form clouds. The rain that falls from these clouds is slightly acidic, making it harmful to living things.

## IMPACT

In the 1980s, scientists noticed that European forests were dying. They tracked the cause of the damage to acid rain. Air pollutants may drift in the wind for hundreds of kilometres. When acid rain falls, it kills trees and drains away into lakes and rivers to harm fish and other water life. This invisible pollution can even erode stone.

▼ *This forest in the Carpathian Mountains of southern Poland has been devastated by the effects of acid rain.*

## WHAT'S THE SOLUTION?

Lime can be dumped in lakes to make them less acidic, but this quick fix can harm water plants. A better solution is to reduce the pollutants at source. Factories can do this by fitting filters to their chimneys and by burning cleaner fuels.

*Sometimes, snow, fog and dust can contain the same toxins as acid rain.*

# Farm chemicals

Farmers spread artificial fertilizers to nourish crops. They also spray **pesticides** to kill weeds and crop-eating insects. However, these farm chemicals harm nature and wildlife.

## EUTROPHICATION

Chemical fertilizers produce bumper crops. But when these substances drain into nearby streams, they cause algae to multiply, smothering the water surface. When these tiny plants die and rot they remove oxygen from the water, which kills fish and water fowl. This problem is called eutrophication.

▼ A farmer sprays a field of growing cotton plants with pesticides in the southern USA.

◄ This osprey may be feeding its chicks with prey poisoned by pesticides absorbed lower down in the food chain.

## FOOD CHAIN IMPACT

Pesticides enter food chains where they are eaten by crop-eating insects. They pass up the chain to birds that eat bugs. The toxins slowly build up in top predators such as falcons and owls, which eat many poisoned prey.

## DDT

In the 1950s, the pesticide DDT was widely used to kill bugs. However, US scientist Rachel Carson found that the chemical was passing up the food chain to weaken the eggshells of predatory birds, so the birds could no longer breed. Her book *Silent Spring* exposed the danger of DDT, leading to the pesticide's ban in Europe and the USA.

# Water pollution

Plants, animals and people cannot live without clean water. However, sources of fresh water everywhere contain pollution. Pollution such as litter on a beach is clearly visible, but toxic chemicals dissolved in water can't be seen and may be deadly.

## RIVER POLLUTION

Many cities are built on rivers that supply fresh water. However, raw sewage and detergent can contaminate fresh water. Poorly regulated farms, industry and mining add more pollutants. In 2000, cyanide from a goldmine poisoned the River Tisza in Hungary, killing fish for 400 kilometres downstream.

▲ The Tisza River in Hungary experienced one of the worst industrial contaminations in modern times.

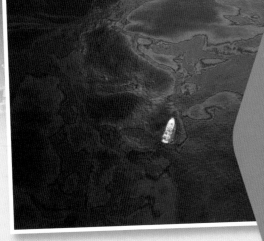

## OIL SPILLS

Oil spills are a major source of ocean pollution. Crude oil kills plankton that provides food for ocean life. It coats birds' feathers and mammals' fur, weakening the waterproofing protection they provide. Seabirds, seals and otters die of cold, starvation or ingested oil. In 2010, an explosion on an oil rig in the Gulf of Mexico created an oil slick that killed 8000 birds, turtles and marine mammals.

▲ An oil spill in the Gulf of Mexico in 2010 covered an area of 10,000 square kilometres.

When rivers flow into the sea, their pollution ends up in the oceans. This can create a 'dead zone' at river estuaries such as the Mississippi Delta, USA. Shallow, sunlit coastal waters are rich in marine life, yet they are also the most polluted part of the oceans.

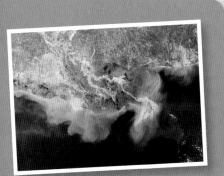

▲ A view of the Mississippi Delta showing river sediment in green. Eighty per cent of ocean pollution comes from rivers.

## SEA DUMPING

For years, rubbish, sewage, chemicals and radioactive waste were dumped at sea. People believed that the oceans were so vast this wouldn't matter, but now we know that dangerous waste is absorbed by marine life such as shrimps and fish, which can then end up on people's plates.

▲ A beach at Dar es Salaam, Tanzania, is covered in washed-up debris.

## CORAL REEFS

Coral reefs are vulnerable to pollution because reef-building polyps only thrive in clean water. Sewage and fertilizers in coastal waters remove oxygen. Silt brought down by rivers can smother the reefs and cloud the water.

▲ Corals require clean water to stay healthy.

# FOOD CHAINS

As on land, water pollution is spread via food chains. Pollutants dissolved in the water are absorbed by microscopic plankton, which provides food for shrimps and molluscs. These are eaten by fish, which pass the poison to seals and seabirds. Top predators like sharks feed on these animals, absorbing high levels of pollutants.

# Tackling pollution

Humans are responsible for almost all pollution on land and in rivers, lakes and oceans. Pollution can be tackled in two main ways. One is to clean up pollution that's already in the environment. But the better option is to prevent the pollution entering the environment in the first place.

## ANTI-POLLUTION LAWS

Environmentalists have been concerned about pollution for over a century. But it wasn't until the 1960s and 70s that governments began to tackle it by passing laws such as the USA's Clean Air and Water Acts. Many countries now have environmental agencies that monitor pollution and make sure industries follow the rules.

## TREATIES

As well as national laws, there are various international agreements to reduce pollution. Many countries have signed the Law of the Sea Treaty, which bans dumping waste at sea. An agreement called the Ramsar Treaty protects wetlands. As a result, many seas, rivers and lakes (such as Lake Bogoria, Kenya, shown above) are now cleaner than they have been for years.

## CAMPAIGNS

Environmental groups such as Greenpeace publicize the dangers of pollution. If a campaign wins popular support, people put pressure on governments to pass laws.

▼ Greenpeace protests outside an oil company in London, UK, against drilling for oil in the Arctic, claiming it threatens the lives of polar bears.

The Gulf of Mexico oil spill has cost $54 billion to clean, and costs continue to rise.

# CAR POLLUTION

Lead used to be added to petrol to make engines run smoothly. But in the 1970s, scientists found that lead from car exhausts was causing brain damage. In many countries, petrol is now lead-free. In the USA, this measure reduced lead levels in the atmosphere by 90 per cent. Devices called catalytic converters are now fitted to cars to reduce other kinds of pollution.

▲ This is the catalytic converter of a diesel engine. It converts pollutants in exhaust gas into less toxic pollutants.

▲ This refinery has attached a 'smoke scrubber' to remove harmful particles.

## POLLUTER PAYS

Industrial pollution can be reduced by fitting filters and scrubbers to power plants and factory chimneys. Many governments now require companies that produce high levels of pollution, whether deliberately or by accident, to pay for the clean-up. This rule is called 'polluter pays'.

## OIL SPILLS

Cleaning up oil spills is very expensive. Spilled oil can be sucked from the sea and beaches. But each oil-soaked animal must be washed individually, and many die. It's better to put in place strict safety rules that make accidents less likely to happen.

## BIOTECHNOLOGY

New, biological ways of tackling pollution are being developed. For example, algae, lichens and bacteria can be used to break down spilled oil, and can even make radioactive waste less harmful.

◀ Volunteers clean a pelican after an oil spill.

# What a waste!

In developed countries, homes, offices, schools, shops, factories and hospitals all produce huge amounts of waste. If not disposed of properly, this can create problems for the environment.

## IN THE BIN

Paper and cardboard make up a third of all household waste. Another third is food waste. The rest is mostly tins, bottles and plastic. Much of what we throw away is packaging, used to wrap food and other items. Most of it goes straight in the bin – a waste of energy and resources.

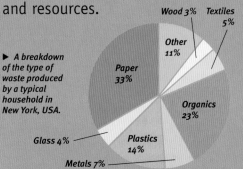

▶ A breakdown of the type of waste produced by a typical household in New York, USA.

Wood 3%  Textiles 5%
Other 11%
Paper 33%
Organics 23%
Glass 4%
Plastics 14%
Metals 7%

▶ A tipper flattens a landfill full of plastic waste.

## LANDFILL

So what happens to our household waste? A lot gets buried in pits called landfills. The mountains of trash are squashed down and covered with soil. But burying waste can cause problems later on. If the site isn't sealed properly, waste can leak out to pollute the air, soil and water. In addition, many countries are running out of space for landfills.

## BURNING WASTE

Waste that isn't buried is either dumped or burned, although dumping at sea is now mostly illegal. Rubbish is burned in furnaces called incinerators. The waste gases given off can be used to generate electricity. However, if the furnace isn't kept hot enough, burning trash creates air pollution.

▲ An incinerator for burning waste in Prague, Czech Republic.

# THROW AWAY SOCIETY

Developed countries have a 'throw-away culture'. Every few years we replace mobiles, computers, tablets and other equipment with the latest models. The old item is usually discarded. This creates a huge amount of unnecessary waste.

▲ Fly-tipping can cause great damage to the environment.

## LITTER

Rubbish dropped on the street or in the countryside creates litter. When someone dumps a large amount of rubbish, it's called fly-tipping. This spoils the environment and harms wildlife.

## A WORLD OF WASTE

Not all countries produce the same amount of waste. Developed countries, such as the UK and USA, produce far more rubbish per person than countries such as India and China. But developed countries also recycle more of their waste (see pages 56–57).

# Does it rot?

Some types of waste biodegrade quickly. But human-made materials, such as metal and plastic, take a long time to decay. Instead they build up and cause problems for the environment.

Tin can
50 years

Foamed plastic cup
50 years

Waxed milk carton
3 months

Apple core
2 months

Toilet roll
2–4 weeks

Glass bottle
1 million years

Disposable nappy
450 years

Wool sock
1–5 years

▲ The rot rates of a number of common household items.

▲ Fruit and vegetable scraps rotting on top of a garden compost heap.

## NATURAL RECYCLING

In nature, plant and animal remains rot quickly with the help of an army of recyclers. Beetles, fungi and bacteria break down dead plants and animals into **organic matter**. The nutrients return to the soil to nourish plants, which are eaten by animals – and so the cycle begins again.

▼ Fungi feeding on a dead tree, recycling its nutrients.

## RATES OF ROTTING

Different materials decay at different rates. Natural substances, such as wool, cloth and wood, rot away quite quickly. However, **synthetic** materials, like plastic, metal and glass, can take centuries to rot, or don't rot away at all.

## COMPOST HEAPS

One way you can cut down on the amount of waste you throw away is by composting food waste. Compost bins are cheap to buy – or you can even make one from wooden crates. Fruit and vegetable peelings, cut flowers, grass and plant clippings can all go on the compost heap. Turn the heap regularly with a fork and in a year or so you will have rich compost with which to fertilize your garden.

# Problems with plastic

Plastic is an amazing material made from oil. The first plastics were made over 150 years ago. Light, strong and tough, plastic is incredibly useful, but it's also long-lasting, which creates a waste disposal problem.

## BEACHES

Plastic waste washes up on beaches the world over. Even remote islands thousands of miles from the nearest city are littered with garbage. Plastic can kill wildlife. Turtles sometimes choke on plastic bags, confusing them with jellyfish. Young seabirds die when their parents feed them plastic pieces they've mistaken for fish.

## CONTAINERS

Plastics are widely used to make all sorts of containers, from flimsy plastic bags to pots, tubs, bottles, bowls and drums. Many foods and liquids are stored in plastic, but while the food and drink is consumed in just a few days, the containers last for decades.

▼ A beach covered with plastic containers and other waste.

## PLASTIC AT SEA

▲ A raft of plastic debris floating on the sea.

A lot of plastic ends up at sea, where some sinks but the rest floats at the surface. Ocean currents then sweep the rubbish into huge rafts of floating debris. The Pacific Ocean contains a vast area of rubbish known as the Great Pacific Garbage Patch spread over 700,000 square kilometres – that's around the size of Texas, USA.

The Pacific Ocean is believed to contain at least 7 million tonnes of rubbish.

# Dealing with waste

In the last 20 years, waste disposal has become a serious problem. As human numbers grow, so does the amount of waste we produce. But it doesn't have to be that way. Many of the materials we throw away are still valuable, and can be reused or recycled in different ways.

## REDUCE, REUSE AND RECYCLE

You can easily cut down on the amount of waste by following the three Rs – Reduce, Reuse and Recycle. This not only reduces waste, but also saves on energy and materials, and reduces pollution.

### REDUCE

Cut down the amount of waste by buying only what you need. Avoid products that use a lot of packaging. Get machinery repaired rather than throwing it out.

### REUSE

Plastic pots and tubs can be turned into flowerpots and pencil holders. Take a reusable cloth bag when you go shopping instead of plastic bags.

### RECYCLE

Many countries collect materials for recycling from homes and the street. Glass, metal, paper, card and some plastics can all be recycled. A wider range of materials can be taken to recycling banks. Books, toys, clothes and crockery can be resold at charity shops.

## PLASTIC

Some plastics can be recycled. A type of plastic known as PET, used to make drinks bottles, can be turned into more bottles, other packaging or even fleece jackets. Other types of plastic are now designed to biodegrade quickly.

▶ *A large pile of bottles lies ready to be recycled.*

## METAL

Cans made of steel and aluminium can be squashed, heated until they melt and then remoulded to make new cans or other metal objects. This process costs a fraction of the amount needed to make new metal.

◀ *All metal food and drink cans can be recycled.*

## GLASS

Waste glass is sorted by colour, smashed into small pieces, reheated and remoulded to make new glass. This saves energy and also reduces the amount of minerals that have to be mined, thereby lowering pollution. Glass can be recycled time and again to make more glass – a process known as closed loop recycling.

**PAPER & CARD**

Recyclable paper is shredded, pulped, pressed and dried to make new paper. Paper can be recycled only five or six times before the fibres get too weak to bond properly.

36

# Climate crisis

**Climate change is one of the most pressing problems facing the world today. Earth's climate is becoming steadily warmer because of air pollution – this is known as global warming. In the past few decades, rising temperatures have begun to affect habitats worldwide.**

## GLOBAL WARMING

Earth's climate has always changed very slowly because of natural changes in the Sun and in Earth's orbit. But now it is warming more quickly. Almost all scientists believe human activities are to blame.

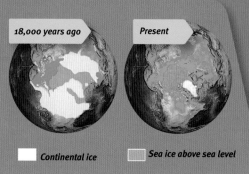

18,000 years ago

Present

☐ Continental ice

☐ Sea ice above sea level

▲ Images showing the extent of ice cover in the northern hemisphere in the last ice age compared to now.

## ICE AGES

Throughout Earth's history, warm periods have been followed by cold eras called ice ages, when ice covered up to a third of Earth's surface. The climate has been slowly getting warmer since the last ice age ended 12,000 years ago, but the rate of warming has increased dramatically in the past century.

## GREENHOUSE EFFECT

Earth's atmosphere contains small amounts of carbon dioxide, methane and water vapour. These gases trap heat close to the planet's surface. They are called **greenhouse gases** because they keep heat from escaping, a bit like how a greenhouse works. For thousands of years, the natural **greenhouse effect** has kept conditions comfortable for life on Earth, but a rise in greenhouse gases could make the atmosphere uncomfortably hot.

**SUN**

▼ Most of the Sun's heat is absorbed by Earth's surface or reflected back out into space (yellow arrows). But greenhouse gases trap some of the heat in the atmosphere (orange arrows).

**ATMOSPHERE**

**EARTH**

**Greenhouse gases**
CO2 and other gases trap the Sun's heat (see page 60).

**Global warming**
Evidence for human-made climate change has been mounting since the 1980s (see page 61).

**Climate change impact**
The effects of global warming could be catastrophic (see pages 62–63).

▲ The tiny air bubbles in this close-up image of an ice core can tell scientists a lot about climate change.

◀ A worker removes an ice core from one of hundreds stored in a US climate research facility.

# EVIDENCE

Scientists learn about past climates by studying samples of ice from the polar regions, known as ice cores. The ice contains air bubbles that show what the climate was like thousands of years ago. Scientists also study growth patterns of ancient trees, which grew faster in warmer years.

# CHANGING CLIMATE

Since 1900, the climate has been warming more quickly than is natural. Scientists believe this is because of increased levels of greenhouse gases in the air. The main greenhouse gas is $CO_2$, which is produced by burning fossil fuels.

# $CO_2$ FACTS

🌍 The levels of carbon dioxide in the atmosphere have increased 30 per cent in the past 50 years.

🌍 Around 15 per cent of the extra carbon dioxide is the result of deforestation.

🌍 In the USA, vehicles produce around 20 per cent of the country's $CO_2$ emissions.

🌍 **Tackling climate change**
There are many things we can do to slow down climate change (see page 64).

🌍 **Alternative energy sources**
There are energy sources that are non-polluting and won't cause climate change (see page 65).

🌍 **Clean energy**
Renewables use natural forces such as water and sunlight to produce energy (see pages 66–67).

# Greenhouse gases

Fossil fuels – coal, oil and natural gas – are the main causes of climate change. As cars, factories and power stations burn these fuels for energy, they pump carbon dioxide into the atmosphere, which is making the planet heat up. Fossil fuels provide 75 per cent of all the energy used in the developed world today.

## FOSSIL FUELS

Coal, oil and gas have been our main energy sources since the Industrial Revolution. As more nations industrialize, more CO2 is released into the atmosphere. The same greenhouse gas is also released when forests are cut down and the wood is burned.

▶ A coal-fired power station in Germany pours steam and greenhouse gases high into the atmosphere on a clear day.

## CARBON PRODUCERS

Developed countries such as the UK and USA produce far more CO2 per person than developing countries such as China and India. We use far more energy for heating, air-conditioning, transport and machines, from fridges to computers. However, China and India have larger populations, and so still produce a lot of greenhouse gas.

# Global warming

Scientists have been warning about the dangers of climate change since the 1980s, but at first there was doubt about the causes. Now scientists agree that global warming is real and climate change is mostly man-made. Rising temperatures are causing polar ice to melt, and making sea levels rise.

## HEATING UP

Temperatures vary from year to year, but there has been an overall upward trend. Temperatures have risen by 0.7°C since 1900. In the polar regions they have risen much faster – by 2.3°C. Every decade since the 1980s has been the warmest on record.

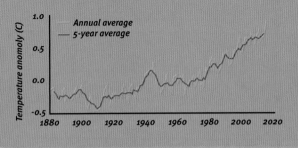

## MONITORING CLIMATE

The Intergovernmental Panel on Climate Change (IPCC) is the main organization that monitors climate. IPCC scientists study data gathered by weather stations all over the world.

## MELTING ICE

Polar ice is not the only ice that is melting. Glaciers on high mountains are also shrinking. Melted land ice is swelling the volume of water in the oceans. This is making sea levels rise.

▼ Antarctic sea ice is seen here melting in early spring, a period when normally sea ice would be extensive and thick.

The area covered by Arctic sea ice is shrinking by about 13.5 per cent each decade.

# Climate change impact

Climate change is affecting environments worldwide. Forests, grasslands, deserts and oceans are heating up. Farmlands and food supplies could be affected as weather patterns change, and rising sea levels could drown coastal cities and islands. Climate change will also have an impact on wildlife.

## OCEAN RISK

Greenhouse gases affect the chemistry of the oceans. Seas and oceans absorb $CO_2$ from the air, which makes the water more acidic. As a result, sea animals, such as clams and lobsters, find it more difficult to build their shells. Global warming could also affect ocean currents.

### EXTREME WEATHER

◀ Hurricanes, such as the one which damaged numerous New York homes in 2012, may be increasing in frequency.

Scientists fear that climate change will influence weather patterns worldwide. Dry areas could be hit by severe droughts, while wet areas could suffer more flooding. Extreme weather events, such as hurricanes, are becoming more common. This suggests that climate change may already be taking effect.

A third of all amphibian species could die out this century as a result of climate change.

# FLOODING

Sea levels rise not only because ice melts but also because warm water expands. Sea levels rose by 20 centimetres in the 20th century. They could rise by 1 to 2 metres or more by 2100. A rise of 2 metres would threaten coastal cities such as New York, Tokyo and Shanghai. Low-lying island nations are particularly vulnerable and could disappear under water.

## WILDLIFE

Living things adapt to slow changes in the environment through evolution. But if conditions change too quickly, many creatures will not cope. Amphibians are threatened by climate change because they lay their eggs in water, and many wetlands are drying out because of global warming.

▲ The low-lying islands of the Maldives, seen here in a satellite view, could be flooded over if sea levels continue to rise.

▲ The sea has become too warm for this reef off the coast of Colombia. It has bleached and the marine life has abandoned it.

## CORAL REEFS

Ocean warming harms coral reefs. Reef-building coral polyps contain tiny plants called algae that supply their food. If temperatures rise, the algae leave the coral, which then turns white and starts to die. This is called bleaching.

## LOST HABITAT

Polar bears may be among the first animals to feel the effects of climate change. These bears do most of their hunting on the Arctic sea ice. If the ice disappears, the bears will lose their main hunting ground.

▼ A polar bear attempts to hunt on thin and fragmented sea ice in the Arctic.

# Tackling climate change

Climate change could affect habitats, wildlife and food supplies worldwide. It's vital that we act now to minimize the effects of global warming. Cutting fossil fuel pollution and switching to other types of fuel will help.

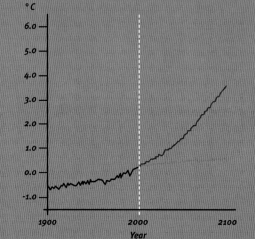

▶ In this graph, the red line shows how much global temperatures will rise by if no action is taken this century. The black line shows how much they rose in the 20th century, while the yellow line is the rise if there is no further increase in emissions.

## NEW AGREEMENT

In 2015, in Paris, 195 world leaders agreed measures to cut carbon pollution. The aim was to keep temperatures from rising beyond 2°C above pre-industrial levels so as to avoid drastic and rapid climate change. This was a success for international cooperation, but developed nations still face a huge challenge.

## CLIMATE CONFERENCES

At Kyoto, Japan, in 1997, a major international conference was held to tackle climate change. Many nations agreed to cut carbon emissions by 2012. This was a step in the right direction, but some nations did not meet their targets.

◀ These tree saplings are ready to plant.

## CUTTING CARBON

**Carbon emissions** can be reduced by fitting filters to power plants that burn fossil fuels. We can also offset carbon pollution by planting and preserving forests because forests absorb $CO_2$. In developed nations, people also need to use far less energy (see pages 68–77).

# Alternative energy sources

Because the burning of fossil fuels is the main cause of climate change, we need to switch to fuels that don't release CO2. Nuclear energy and hydrogen are two alternative energy sources.

## ACCIDENTS

In 1986, an accident at the Chernobyl nuclear plant in Ukraine spread radioactive pollution over a large part of Europe. In 2011, a tsunami (giant wave) damaged a Japanese nuclear plant, which leaked radiation into the sea. These accidents convinced many people that nuclear energy is not a safe option.

▼ Today, Chernobyl, the town in Ukraine in which the nuclear plant was located, is a ghost town.

## NUCLEAR ENERGY

Nuclear energy is made by splitting atoms of the mineral uranium in a nuclear reactor. This process, called fission, does not make greenhouse gases. But it does produce radioactive waste that remains dangerous for centuries. No one has worked out how to dispose of this waste safely, so it is just buried. Like fossil fuels, stocks of uranium are also limited. One day they will run out, so these fuels are **non-renewable**.

France is one of Europe's lowest CO2 producers – three quarters of its energy is nuclear.

## HYDROGEN

Fuel cells harness energy released from the reaction between oxygen and hydrogen to produce electricity. The only waste product is water. Liquid hydrogen, a pressurized gas, can also be used to power vehicles.

◄ An experimental fuel-cell car in 2014.

# Clean energy

'Clean' energy sources use natural forces such as sunlight, wind and flowing water. These technologies do not produce greenhouse gases and are renewable, but there are still some drawbacks.

## WIND

Wind energy has been used for centuries. Modern wind turbines have thin blades which rotate to drive a generator. However, each turbine produces relatively little energy, and wind farms can only be sited in windy places. Wind farms at sea work well, but are expensive to build.

## BIOFUELS

Biofuels are fuels generated from crops, plants or animal waste. The waste rots in special tanks to produce methane, which can be burned for energy. Biofuels are **renewable** but produce some greenhouse gases. In addition, growing biofuels takes up land that could be used for crops.

▼ *A field of bright yellow rapeseed, a commonly used biofuel.*

◄ *Solar panels like these work best in countries that enjoy a lot of sunshine.*

## SOLAR

The Sun is Earth's main energy source. Its energy can be harnessed in several ways. Solar panels on roofs provide heat. Photovoltaic cells convert light to electricity. Solar energy can also be used to power small devices such as torches. At present, solar technology is fairly expensive, and only works well on a large scale in hot, sunny climates.

*Renewable sources currently provide just a fraction of the world's total energy.*

# HYDROPOWER

The energy of fast-flowing water can be turned into electricity. In a hydroelectric plant, the water turns turbines connected to a generator. While no greenhouse gases are produced, the dams built to regulate the flow of water create large reservoirs, which can destroy habitats.

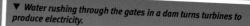
▼ Water rushing through the gates in a dam turns turbines to produce electricity.

◄ A large wind farm in California, USA.

## TIDES AND WAVES

A tidal station uses a large dam called a barrage built across a river estuary. The tidewater is trapped to spin turbines linked to a generator, but the barrage can harm coastal ecosystems. Free-standing generators can also be built out to sea to harness tidal currents. Waves contain huge amounts of energy, but scientists are still working out how best to harness wave power.

▼ A free-standing generator shown with its turbines raised out of the water.

## GEOTHERMAL

Hot rocks below ground in volcanic areas can be used to heat water and generate electricity. But some greenhouse gases are produced, and this technology only works in regions with active volcanoes.

▼ Naturally occurring steam billows from a geothermal plant in Iceland – a very volcanically active country.

# Looking after the environment

A healthy environment is vital for all living things, including people. We rely on nature for oxygen, food, water, energy and other resources. It's crucial that we learn to take care of the planet to preserve these resources for the future. This is known as **sustainability**.

## EXPLORING SUSTAINABILITY

Earth has abundant food, water, timber and minerals. But these resources aren't limitless. If we take too much now, there will be less in the future. That's where sustainability comes in. It means using natural resources carefully, to preserve stocks for the future.

▼ *Illegal logging has decimated this forest in Tasmania, Australia.*

▶ *Pacific bluefin tuna is sold at a market in Japan. Overfishing has seen the numbers of this fish decline in recent years.*

▲ *This rubber tree in Sri Lanka is being tapped sustainably.*

## SUSTAINABLE FORESTRY

Forests can be managed sustainably by selecting trees for felling rather than clear-cutting, and by planting saplings to replace trees that are felled. Rubber, nuts and fruits can be harvested without having to cut down the trees.

*Thirty per cent of all the food produced each year is thrown away uneaten.*

| 🌍 **Sustainability** | 🌍 **Saving water** | 🌍 **A fair share for all** | 🌍 **Food issues** |
|---|---|---|---|
| The future of the planet depends on us using resources sustainably (see above). | Some areas have enough water while others suffer shortages (see page 70). | Developed countries use the majority of Earth's resources (see page 71). | Supermarkets have an enormous impact on the environment (see page 72). |

# ECOLOGICAL FOOTPRINT

Scientists use the term 'ecological footprint' to describe human impact on world resources. In 2014, the global ecological footprint was 1.6 planet Earths. That means we are using up Earth's resources 1.6 times faster than nature can replace them.

## SUSTAINABILITY FACTS

- Between 2000 and 2010, 52,000 square kilometres of forest were cleared, an area the size of Costa Rica.

- Each year, 131 million tonnes of fish are caught and used for food, more than the oceans can sustain.

- The average person gets through two trees' worth of paper products a year.

- Across the globe, around one million new plastic bags are used every minute.

- Around 25 million plastic bottles are thrown away every hour in the USA.

## WHY PROTECT THE PLANET?

Even if you live in the centre of a city, you cannot survive without nature. People once saw nature as something to be tamed and dominated. Now we know it's vital to look after the environment. The future of the planet is in our hands and depends on choices we make today.

▶ The Siberian tiger is being reintroduced to the wild by conservationists. Its numbers were severely depleted by hunting and loss of habitat during the 20th century.

**GM crops**
The use of genetically modified crops has prompted a global debate (see page 73).

**Sustainable farming**
Organic farmers produce chemical-free food (see page 74).

**Sustainable cities**
Cities have a significant and growing impact on the environment (see page 75).

**How can I help?**
There are many things we can all do to help the environment (see pages 76–77).

# Saving water

Clean water is essential for all living things. Unfortunately, fresh water supplies are not evenly distributed across the planet. Some regions receive abundant rainfall. There may even be too much rain, leading to flooding. But large parts of Earth's surface have the opposite problem – water is very scarce.

## BOOM AND BUST

Scientists have worked out that every person needs 50 litres of water a day for drinking, washing and cooking. People in developed countries use far more than that – up to 500 litres a day. In many African countries people get by on just 10 litres a day. Across the world 780 million people are without clean water, and nearly 2.5 billion lack proper sanitation.

▲ *Watering golf courses accounts for 0.5 per cent of all the water used in the USA every day.*

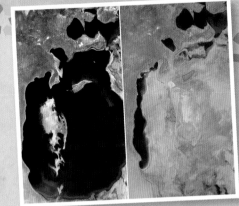

▲ *On the left is a satellite image of the Aral Sea in 1989, and on the right, the same lake in 2014.*

## SHRINKING SEA

The        Sea in western Asia was once the world's fourth-largest lake. But so much water has been diverted for farming that the lake has shrunk to a fraction of its former size.

▲ *Abandoned fishing boats on the dried-up lake bed.*

# A fair share for all

By 2030 there may be 9 billion people on the planet. As numbers rise, more and more land wil be needed for farming. Earth has enough fertile land for everyone on the planet, but resources aren't divided equally.

## FEAST...

People in developed countries consume about 60 per cent of the world's food, leaving little for the rest of the planet. They enjoy a varied diet, eating a lot of meat, dairy and sweet, fatty foods such as cakes and pastries. As a result, **obesity** is a growing problem. People in developed countries also waste a lot of food.

## ...AND FAMINE

In developing countries, people have a far less varied diet. Much of the fertile land there is used to grow food and rear livestock to feed people in rich countries. The land that is left to grow food for local people is often dry and stony. The result is that many people don't have enough to eat.

**SOLUTIONS**

The United Nations and charities such as Oxfam are working to reduce poverty and hunger. Food aid is given to people at risk of starvation, but the real solution is to improve farming in developing countries, so people can grow enough food to be able to feed themselves.

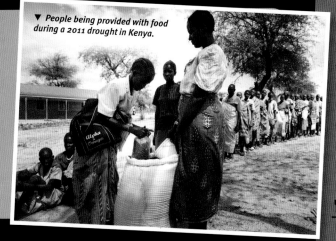

▼ *People being provided with food during a 2011 drought in Kenya.*

# Food issues

In developed countries most of the food is bought from supermarkets. These stores offer a wide range of products grown all over the world. This means people can enjoy exotic foods such as bananas all year round, but sourcing food from faraway places has an impact on the environment.

## FOOD MILES

Much of the food sold in supermarkets has travelled thousands of kilometres. This distance is called food miles. Transporting food across the world by planes, ships and trucks is a major source of greenhouse gases. Buying locally grown foods in season is kinder to the environment.

## FAIR TRADE

Supermarkets buy much of their food from developing countries. Quite often they pay growers a low price. This keeps prices low for customers, but means that many farmers in developing countries earn very little money. The fair trade movement offers farmers a fair price for their crops. Buying fair trade goods, such as bananas, tea and coffee, helps farmers in the developing world.

▲ Meat from New Zealand sheep is exported all over the world.

▲ Standard-sized fruit and vegetables for sale in a supermarket.

## PERFECT PRODUCE

Supermarkets often only sell fruit and vegetables of a standard size and shape, that are free from blemishes. Farm produce that doesn't meet these requirements is rejected. This encourages farmers to use more chemicals, and also wastes a lot of food.

# GM crops

Scientists can create new varieties of plants and animals by transferring **genes** from one living thing to another. This technique is called genetic modification, and the new varieties are known as genetically modified organisms (GMOs). This **biotechnology** has amazing potential, but some people feel it's a danger to the natural world.

## USES

Biotech companies use genetic modification (GM) to create new strains of crops that can resist frost or drought. Fruits such as tomatoes have been modified to taste better and last longer. Other crops contain added vitamins or genes that allow them to be sprayed with very powerful pesticides.

▼ *People examine a field of insect-resistant GM maize (corn) in Kenya, Africa.*

## AROUND THE WORLD

GM crops are widely grown in the USA and Canada. Most processed foods now contain modified crops such as maize and soybeans. But GM foods there aren't labelled. GM crops are carefully controlled or banned altogether in Australia, New Zealand and much of Europe, and GM foods must be labelled.

Around 88 per cent of the maize eaten in the USA has been genetically modified.

## DEBATE

Scientists are divided about GM. Biotech companies say GM is only an extension of breeding techniques that have been used for centuries. They claim GM will help to solve world hunger. But some ecologists fear GMOs could spread to other crops and wild plants, possibly damaging them.

▼ *An anti-GM march in Vancouver, Canada.*

# Sustainable farming

Modern intensive farming involves chemicals which produce pollution and harm wildlife. Organic farming and free-range livestock farming are alternative methods that are kinder to nature and more sustainable.

▶ *A farmer engaged in intercropping –growing two crops (coffee and tomatoes) side by side to control pests and return nutrients to the soil.*

## ORGANIC FARMING

Organic farming is a method of farming without chemicals. Organic farmers use manure and crop waste to fertilize the soil instead of chemical fertilizers. Different crops are grown in fields each year. This practice, called crop rotation, helps to restore nutrients. These farmers encourage pest-eating predators such as ladybirds to control insects, rather than spraying with pesticide.

▲ *An organically grown cucumber and tomato (left) compared to the intensively farmed GM alternatives.*

## FREE RANGE

Most livestock farmers use intensive methods to rear their stock. Animals are kept indoors and are fed medicines and chemicals called hormones to speed up their growth. Free-range animals are allowed to roam more freely and aren't fed medicines or hormones.

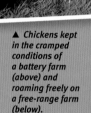

▲ *Chickens kept in the cramped conditions of a battery farm (above) and roaming freely on a free-range farm (below).*

# Sustainable cities

The rapid growth of cities causes many problems for the environment. Many modern cities are congested, polluted and overcrowded. Making cities more sustainable helps to reduce our impact on the natural world.

▼ An electric-powered bus in Germany.

## POLLUTION

City traffic causes congestion, smog and greenhouse gases. City councils can reduce pollution by improving public transport so people use their cars less. In future, public transport could run on non-polluting fuels such as hydrogen.

▲ Recycling bins for plastic bottles (left), food and drink cans (centre) and waste paper (right).

## WASTE

Waste and litter are a big problem in many cities. Councils can help by providing recycling facilities and encouraging people to recycle. In some city districts in developing countries, waste is not collected. But materials such as card and metal are valuable, so a lot of waste is recycled.

## ENERGY

Cities use huge amounts of resources, including energy. New housing estates and office buildings can be made more environmentally friendly by being well insulated. Efficient heating can be powered by renewables such as solar power.

▼ This new home has had solar panels installed on its roof to save energy.

It takes the same amount of energy to recycle 20 cans as it does to produce 1 new one.

# How can I help?

Conservation has come a long way in the last century. But more action is urgently needed to keep the planet green, leafy and unpolluted. Governments, businesses and industries have a big role to play, but so do ordinary people. We can all make choices to help the environment.

▲ *Always remember to switch off lights if you no longer need them.*

▶ *Switch the TV off rather than leave it on standby to save energy.*

▶ *If possible, try to dry clothes outdoors on a washing line.*

## REDUCING ENERGY

Excessive use of energy is harming the environment and producing greenhouse gases. Reduce the amount of energy you use with these tips:

- 🌍 Turn off lights when they're not needed.
- 🌍 Computers and TVs use energy in standby mode. Switch them off when they're not in use.
- 🌍 Buy low-energy lightbulbs, which use far less energy than ordinary bulbs.
- 🌍 Put on a sweater and turn the central heating down a notch if you are cold.
- 🌍 Dry clothes outside on a washing line instead of using a tumble drier.

# FOOD AND SHOPPING

To reduce waste, you could choose products with less packaging. Buying local fruits and vegetables in season will save energy and resources, as will eating less meat. Indeed, land used to provide meat for five people could feed up to 150 if sown with crops.

## SAVING WATER

Using water carefully helps to preserve stocks of fresh water. Try these tips:
- 🌍 Take a shower instead of a bath.
- 🌍 Don't leave taps dripping, and get leaks fixed quickly.
- 🌍 Turn off the tap while you brush your teeth.
- 🌍 Only use the dishwasher and washing machine with a full load.
- 🌍 Use a watering can, not a hose, to water the garden.
- 🌍 Report any water leaks you see when you're outdoors.

## CONSERVATION

To help preserve the environment, you could join an environmental group such as the World Wide Fund for Nature, Friends of the Earth or Greenpeace. Alternatively, you could raise funds for conservation causes by doing a sponsored hike, swim or cycle ride.

## HELP WILDLIFE

You could make your garden wildlife-friendly by putting out food for birds. Planting wildflowers will attract insects such as bees and butterflies. Perhaps you could ask your parents if you can dig a small pond to help frogs and other water life.

▶ *Putting up bird boxes can help the local wildlife.*

## TRAVEL

Vehicles produce at least a fifth of all greenhouse gases. Using public transport produces far less emissions per person than going by car. Can you travel to school by bus or train, or can you walk, cycle or share a ride?

◀ *Cycling not only protects the environment, it also helps you to keep fit.*

# GLOSSARY

**ADAPTATION**
The process of becoming better suited to the environment.

**ATMOSPHERE**
The layer of gases surrounding Earth.

**BIODIVERSITY**
The variety of living things in a habitat.

**BIOME**
A huge habitat dominated by a particular type of vegetation, such as rainforest.

**BIOSPHERE**
All the life on Earth as well as all the places that contain life.

**BIOTECHNOLOGY**
Technology that uses living things.

**CARBON EMISSIONS**
The release of carbon dioxide gas.

**CLIMATE**
The general weather conditions in an area over a long period of time.

**DECIDUOUS**
Trees that drop their leaves in autumn, and grow new ones in spring.

**ECOLOGIST**
Someone who studies the environment.

**ECOSYSTEM**
A community of interacting living things and their environment.

**EROSION**
The gradual destruction of something, such as a rock, by natural forces such as flowing water or ice.

**EVOLUTION**
The theory that explains how species gradually change over time.

**FISHERY**
An area where lots of fish live and are fished intensively.

**FOSSIL FUELS**
Coal and oil. These fuels are made of fossilized plants and animals.

**GENES**
Tiny structures in cells that control how an organism develops.

**GREENHOUSE EFFECT**
The warming effect caused by certain gases in the air.

**GREENHOUSE GASES**
Gases that cause global warming.

**HERBIVORE**
An animal that eats only plants.

**IGNEOUS ROCK**
Rock formed when magma (molten rock) solidifies beneath Earth's surface.

## INDUSTRIAL REVOLUTION

A period from the mid 18th to the mid 19th century when several countries saw a rapid rise in the number of industries, fuelled by the development of new steam-powered machinery.

## INTRODUCED SPECIES

A species that has been brought to an environment by people.

## METAMORPHIC ROCK

A rock formed when heat and pressure are applied to existing rocks (igneous or sedimentary) deep underground.

## NON-RENEWABLE

A resource that cannot be replenished once it's been used up.

## NORTHERN HEMISPHERE

The northern half of the Earth.

## OBESITY

The state of being grossly overweight.

## ORGANIC MATTER

Natural waste made of plants and animals.

## ORGANISM

A living thing.

## PESTICIDE

A poisonous chemical used to kill weeds or crop-eating insects.

## PHOTOSYNTHESIS

The process through which plants make their own food using carbon dioxide, nutrients and sunlight.

## RADIATION

Energy emitted in the form of waves or rays.

## RENEWABLE

Resources that can be continually renewed, such as sunlight and water.

## SEDIMENTARY ROCK

Rock formed by the slow build-up of small pieces of rock, minerals and organic matter.

## SPECIES

A group of living organisms that share genes and physical characteristics, and can reproduce.

## SUSTAINABILITY

The practice of using resources responsibly to ensure they are still available for future generations.

## SYNTHETIC

Something that is manmade rather than occurring naturally.

## WEATHERING

The wearing away of something, such as a rock, via the action of wind, rain and other weather conditions.

# INDEX

Picture credits (t=top, b=bottom, l=left, r=right, c=centre, fc=front cover, bc=back cover, i=image)

All images courtesy of Dreamstime unless otherwise indicated:
*iStock.com*: 42–43c. *NASA*: fc line 2 i5, fc line 3 i1, fc line 3 i2, fc line 5 i2, fc line 6 i4, fc line 7 i2, 6–7c, 43cr, 44tl, 45cr, 48t. *Public Domain*: 21br, 26b, 33l, 51bl, 59cl, 63tr, 67cr, 70bl. *United States Air Force*: fc line 6 i2. fc line 7 i5. *Wikimedia Commons*: fc line 1 i1 Diorit, fc line 1 i3 Onderwijsgek, fc line 1 i4 Steve Wilson, fc line 1 i6 Eviatar Bach, fc line 2 i1 Richard Ling, fc line 2 image 4 Cyrus Read USGS, fc line 3 i3 Robert Jack, fc line 3 i4 Jason Auch, fc line 3 i5 Nickpdx, fc line 3 i6 Tomas Castelazo, fc line 4 i2 Joe Mastroianni, fc line 4 i3 Arne Hückelheim, fc line 5 i1 Nepenthes, fc line 5 i3 Whit Welles, fc line 5 i4 Cai Tjeenk Willink, fc line 5 i5 Kpnc Knpenk, fc line 6 i1, fc line 6 i3 Jorge medina, fc line 6 i5 Jessie Eastland, fc line 7 i1 InvictaHOG, fc line 7 i3 Dirk Beyer, fc line 7 i5 Malene Thyssen, 19c Doug Smith, 29br Bill Bouton, 31tl Charles H. Smith, 31c BazzaDaRambler, 48bl kris krüg, 49cr Loranchet, 59t CSIRO, 73br Dave Hoisington/CIMMYT, 73bl Rosalee Yagihara, 74t Neil Palmer, 74 bl Aenpnha, 75tr Lord Alpha.